SUCCESSFUL WINDSURFING

Clive Boden

Illustrations by Alan Batley

SACKVILLE
BOOKS

First published in 1989
by Sackville Books Ltd
Stradbroke, Suffolk, England

Text © Clive Boden
© Sackville Books Limited 1989

Designed and produced by Sackville Design Group Limited
Art Editor: Rolando Ugolini
Editor: Nick Bevan

British Library Cataloguing in Publication Data
Boden, Clive
Successful windsurfing. — (Sackville sports clinic)
1. Windsurfing
I. Title
797.3'3

ISBN 0 948615 25 7

Typeset by Micropress, Halesworth, Suffolk, England.
Reproduction by BPCC Bury Studios, Bury St Edmunds, Suffolk, England

Printed and bound by Serif Cowells plc, Ipswich, Suffolk.

Contents

	Introduction	4
1.	Choosing the right equipment	5
2.	Launching your board from the beach	22
3.	Using a harness	27
4.	Getting on to a plane	30
5.	Sailing on a long board	32
6.	Foot steering	38
7.	The carved gybe	40
8.	Water starts	46
9.	Advanced windsurfing	52
10.	Wave-jumping	66
11.	Wave-riding	76
	Glossary	80

Introduction

I can remember sitting on a beach in Yugoslavia in 1974 watching a crazy German sailing on what looked like a front door, with an old handkerchief for a sail. He streaked off across the bay, tried to turn around, fell in, took about ten minutes to get up and streaked off in the opposite direction, only to take another ten minute wipe out.

Four years later, bored on a beach in Ibiza, I enrolled in a class teaching the new sport taking Europe by storm — windsurfing. I then spent hours on my board tethered to a buoy like an aquatic goat. I returned to England and joined one of the early gravel pit fleets springing up around west London.

Since then, my career as a professional advertising photographer has allowed me to travel to many parts of the world. It was no coincidence that some assignments ended up being shot in prime windsurfing venues. I was fortunate enough to go to Hawaii at the beginning of the short board revolution and meet young kids who are now windsurfing superstars. One such friend was the late Angus Chater, one of the great innovators in the sport and a brilliant photographer. Our friendship led to several projects together such as brochure work for the first waterproof walkman for Sony. Eventually we produced *The Windsurfing Funboard Handbook* together, the first funboard book in the UK and USA, selling over 100,000 copies. Subsequently I have photographed a skiing book and become a snow board enthusiast.

This book assumes that the reader has undergone a basic approved windsurfing course which no book can substitute. I was interested in producing a book utilising the help of video to produce accurate illustration references. *Successful Windsurfing* will describe the functions of each element of your board and rig and explain how to maximise their potential in performance sailing. The step-by-step illustrations go through the whole spectrum of modern sailboarding manoeuvres from simple foot steering to killer loops as performed by the world's top sailors.

I would like to thank all the people who helped produce *Successful Windsurfing* and especially my wife, Lesley for all the waiting around in airports over the years for windsurfers that never arrived on time.

CHAPTER ONE

Choosing the right equipment

When sailboarding first started to become popular, choosing the right board and rig was simple. There was only the original 'Windsurfer' board and a couple of imitations. You had a large standard sail and, if you were really keen, you invested in a small 'storm sail' for when the wind blew hard.

You would have to set your small sail on your standard mast and boom, which were totally incompatible in size — and as you sailed off, you would require the strength of Rambo to control the board in the gusts. It was fun — but not smooth, performance sailing. The original sailboard was great to handle on flat water and in light to moderate winds, but it was difficult in strong winds and waves.

In places such as Hawaii, pioneers started developing boards with foot straps, retractable daggerboards, or even no daggerboards at all. Boards became smaller, similar to surfboards, to the point where they had so little volume, they had to be kept on the plane, or the weight of the sailor would sink it. These boards, known as sinkers, were fine in the hands of the local Hawaiian experts, but were too advanced for sailing techniques in Europe at the time.

Since those early days there has been rapid development in the design of boards and rigs. Luckily for those sailors coming into the sport now, the early experimentation and mistakes have been consolidated, and now many manufacturers produce excellent, well tried and tested equipment.

Types of Board

You probably started to learn your basic sailing on a sailboard which was very buoyant. This made it easy to learn to uphaul the rig and sail a course on flat water and in light winds. Unfortunately, as the wind grows stronger, this type of board becomes more difficult to handle. If you want to advance to sailing in stronger winds (force four and above) you should next consider a more refined craft — an all-round funboard.

The All-round Funboard

This is a version of the basic sailboard, refined to give improved handling qualities. It measures between 3.2 and

3.8 m, and is up to 62 cm wide with a maximum volume of 230 litres. It has two sets of front foot straps and two positions for the rear straps. These keep your feet in contact with the board, so you have more control at speed. The front set of each pair is for beating upwind, and the rear set of each pair for reaching. It has a narrow, retractable daggerboard which you use in the down position for beating upwind, and fully retracted into the hull for reaching. A sliding mast track is used in the front position to make sure the maximum length of hull pushes through the water for good up-wind performance, while you use it in the rear position to reduce the 'wetted' area for good planing on the rear of the board, helped by a large skeg at the rear. The tail of the board is a pin-tail or rounded pin-tail shape to allow foot steering.

Although many of the larger all-round funboards are around 3.7 m long, and still fulfil all the fundamental requirements, you may wish to consider a board which is shorter in length. The shortest which still has the advantage of the retractable daggerboard for up-wind sailing is about 320 cm long. If you feel confident about progressing quickly and want to get into short-board manoeuvres, this type of board will give you a good start.

You might choose a short, all-round funboard with the advantage of a retractable daggerboard if there are strong currents for sailing around the coast. For lake sailing you would probably prefer a longer all-round funboard — especially if you are competitive. Then you should consider a course racing funboard.

The Course Racing Funboard
This board is a highly-tuned version of the all-round funboard, developed from the World Cup Team's racing boards.

The course racing funboard must be able to beat upwind, reach and gybe like the all-round funboard — but at greater speed. On the other hand, they are not expected to jump. The length varies from 370-380 cm, with a maximum width of about 65 cm. Although these boards are long, with a volume of 200-240 litres, high-tech construction can get the weight of these boards down to a remarkable 13 kg. As with the all-round funboard, there are two rear footstraps and two pairs of front straps, but this time there is an additional front set, set forward parallel to the line of the board. These straps, in conjunction with the sliding mast track forward, help to push the maximum length of board on to the waterline. The thick rails in the middle section of the board, along with high volume up front, allow the rider to dig in the leeward rail for lateral resistance, so producing excellent up-wind performance.

The daggerboard is specially shaped larger for improved performance, and is fitted with rubber gaskets to seal the slot into which it retracts.

When you pull the mast track right back, the board planes on the rear section so that it acts like a short board. The tail section has much less volume, with hard rails and a 'V' in the underside. This last feature allows you to gybe well which, on a board this long, must be done right on the tail.

The underwater profile of the board has a double concave, which gives lift and early planing ability. The tail is a round pin-tail shape.

Short boards

Once you're competent, to appreciate the real excitement of funboarding, you need to progress to a short board. Then, when you get a decent wind speed (force 4 and upwards), you can discover the thrills of making perfectly-carved turns, you can ride the waves, jump in the air and even pull off the ultimate trick of today — the aerial loop!

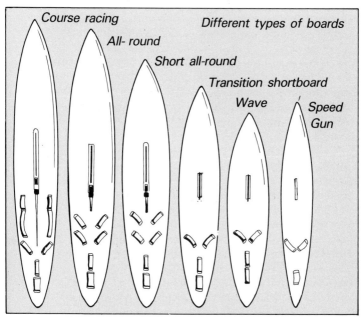

Course racing
All-round
Short all-round
Different types of boards
Transition shortboard
Wave
Speed
Gun

By the very fact of its reduced size, buoyancy has to be a fundamental consideration. You measure the volume of a board in litres and the relationship between the weight in kilos of the sailor with his wet suit, board and rig against the volume of the board in litres determines whether the board can be uphauled or has to be water started. The degree of buoyancy in boards is often graded in three categories — it is either a floater, a marginal or a sinker. Floaters are high-volume short boards which most sailors can manage to uphaul, whereas sinkers have a low volume and can only be water started. A board would be termed marginal when you can subtract the weight of the boardrig and rider in kilos from the quoted volume of the hull in litres and the difference is less than about 10 litres. This would mean that you could stand on the board, but you would have to water start it, and it would require a wind strength of force 4-5 to perform well. Obviously, because the question of floatation is related to your body weight, one man's floater could be another man's sinker.

Marginal boards

Most manufacturers offer a range of short boards. As a good introduction to this area of sailing, go for a board of 295 cm in length. You would describe this as a 'transition' board (from long to sinker-sized boards). A light sailor could most probably uphaul it, albeit with some difficulty in heavy weather — but it would rate as a marginal for most other heavier sailors.

A 295 would have a width of 60-61 cm and a volume of 115-120 litres, and would be fitted with one set of front straps and two rear positions. The mast foot is in a slot which allows some adjustment before you begin sailing but, unlike the sliding tracks on race boards, you can't move it while sailing.

This length of board has no daggerboard and would have a single rear skeg, possibly with small slots for 'thruster' fins forward to either side.

The tail shapes have varied a lot in the past, but have now generally settled down to pin-tails, with or without 'wingers': all are mainly single or multi-channelled. This gives good acceleration and planing, and is excellent for reaching on slalom-type courses. Hence this type of 270-295 cm board is often called a slalom or slalom/wave board, deriving its shape from World Cup Slalom racing boards, for which the course is set back and forth across the wind and sometimes through surf.

The sinker

The sinker is the smallest of the short boards and requires very competent — if not advanced — sailing techniques. I would not recommend using one until you can water start and gybe in strong winds and heavy seas. Many think of it as the ultimate funboard as its reduced length and volume make it handle better as the wind gets stronger (force 6 and above) — on the other hand a longer 295 starts to get more tricky. Conversely, when the wind drops the sinker becomes hopeless. This type of board is good for wave-riding and jumping and slalom in very high winds. It can be as short as 240 cm long, but a popular size is around 260 cm long and 56-57 cm wide. The mast foot track arrangement is similar to that of a 295, but the short board may have only one rear foot-strap position.

I need to explain tail, rail and underwater shapes more fully for this specialized type of board — it is covered on pages 11-14.

Speed gun

There is one last, very specialized type of short board which is worth mentioning. There has been a lot of interest in the last few years in speed trials — especially as sailboards now dominate the world sailing speed record. Speed boards have developed from the 'Waimea Gun' — a long, thin, drawn-out surf-board, used to ride the waves of Waimea Bay on the north shore of Oahu in the Hawaiian Islands. These boards are about 275 cm long, only around 45 cm wide, very light — and go incredibly fast! A short-board mast foot track is standard, with a single rear fin and one set each of front and rear straps. Hull shapes have tended to be very experimental, but at present seem to be single concave with planing rails.

Method of construction

There are two principal methods of constructing a board — they are either custom-made or moulded.

Custom

A custom board is an individually designed, hand-crafted board, shaped with an electric plane from a polyurethane or polystyrene block known as a 'blank'. This has wooden ribs called stringers down its centre to give it rigidity. After the 'shaper' has achieved the required dimensions and detailing, the next stage is to decorate the blank by spraying airbrush designs over it. The hull is then laminated with a skin of glass-fibre, using resin. Hours of polishing finally acquire a gloss finish. Then foot straps, skeg boxes and mast tracks can all be fitted according to individual requirements.

This method of construction is an extension of the techniques used by surfboard builders before sailboards were even invented. Therefore many of today's shapers come from this background and some now enjoy international status and recognition. Working with top professional sailors, these shapers can convert the riders' ideas and suggestions into workable boards. These boards, in turn, can become the master copy or 'plug' for the moulds for production boards. I cannot see any way to supercede this type of research and development, although some mechanical, computerized shaping equipment has been introduced.

Moulded construction
A moulded board, although its design would have originated from a custom board, is manufactured in quite a different way, which allows mass-production. The main techniques are: **(1) Polyethylene:** This type of board is heavy and flexible but has the advantage of being tough and inexpensive to produce, and therefore to buy. **(2) Glass-fibre:** These boards are inexpensive, and quite light and stiff. Unfortunately, the outer skin is not very durable, and the join line can become a problem area. **(3) ASA and polyurethane:** Again, these are inexpensive but quite heavy at the cost of durability.

Composite construction
Leading manufacturers now seem to be favouring this complex, high-tech method using an EPS (extruded polystyrene) core for minimum weight, wrapped in fibreglass cloth (sometimes reinforced with Kevlar), a second layer of cloth and finally an ASA outer skin. Some of these boards now even have hard foam stringers. The advantages of this kind of construction are lightness, stiffness and good durability. The big disadvantage is the high retail cost. Obviously this is the best type of moulded board to buy if you can afford it.

Custom or moulded?

Custom boards used to be an expensive luxury, but nowadays prices seem to have stabilized. Moulded short boards are now as stiff as custom boards and can be up to 2 kg lighter for the same length. A custom board is quite fragile and needs careful looking after. A composite moulded board is much more resilient to knocks — and a polyethylene board is virtually indestructible!

If you are looking at a long board — 3 m or over, I don't see any choice but a good moulded board. When you get to 295 cm or less, the choice is more difficult. In a good moulded board you should be sure of quality of manufacture (backed by a guarantee and a good resale value). A good moulded board will have a tried-and-tested design. However, you won't be getting a unique, hand-crafted board with your own design features incorporated, and the finish can't even start to compare with the fantastic looks of a custom board.

If you do invest in a custom board, there is no reason why, if you are careful, it shouldn't last well, provided that you make simple repairs to relatively minor 'dings'. People still claim that you cannot achieve the same degree of fine detail on the shaping (especially of the rails) on a moulded board as you can on a custom one, although they are getting very much more comparable now. If you always sail in an area where there is a good local custom board-maker, he will know the local conditions and be able to build a board suitable for those conditions, whereas a moulded board is inevitably likely to be a compromise.

Board dynamics

Length, width and thickness
We have already discussed lengths of boards and their relationship to body-weight and floatation. Generally speaking, the longer the board, the more stable it is — but the harder to manoeuvre. There is no point in buying a sinker unless you regularly sail in winds of force 5 and over.

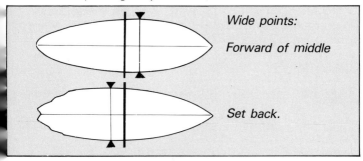

Wide points:

Forward of middle

Set back.

Board width and the siting of the widest point along the length of the board are very important factors. A narrow board which has the widest point forward produces a long, drawn-out tail shape, as on a speed board. This means the board has very little buoyancy and is hopeless in anything but strong winds — but when it does blow, it has so little wetted area, and therefore friction, that it is incredibly fast. So narrow boards are only suitable for high winds. On the other hand, a wider board will give more buoyancy and begin planing in less wind. A narrow board turns around a wide arc, but if the widest point is set further back, you can pivot on the tail section to give sharper turns. In general, the wide point should be forward for strong winds and further back for moderate winds.

Just as with considerations of width, a board needs to be thinner for stronger winds and thicker for lighter winds. In order to turn the board, you need to sink the rails. If they are too thick, you won't be able to sink them and the tail will bounce around. On the other hand, if the tail is too thin, you will sink too much and stall.

Scoop and rocker

The scoop is the amount by which the nose of the board turns up, and the rocker is the degree of tail lift. Within reason, less scoop makes a faster board on flat water — in waves, however, you need more scoop.

Likewise, less rocker in the tail makes for a faster board on flat water, but makes it more difficult to turn in the waves and for gybing. The degree of rocker is usually a compromise between the requirements for going fast and turning well.

Rails

Rails are the side of the hull and their shape and profile vary along the board's length.

Hard, thin, turned-down rails (a) are good at speed and release water cleanly, allowing the tail to dig in during a turn or when cutting through chop at the nose of the board.

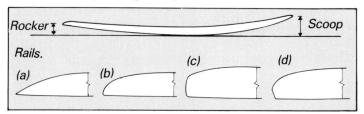

Rounded rails (b) allow the water to flow up, hugging the rails, making it easier to turn in lighter winds.

Slab-sided rails (c) have a vertical edge, good for light winds and providing floatation during slower turns.

A tucked edge (d) is a combination of soft and hard rails. A hard water-release edge at the bottom of the rail stops the water from wrapping around and promotes quick planing. But when you bank the board into a turn, it comes off the water-release edge and on to the tuck, sticking to the water and improving turning capabilities.

Although the rails change from hard at the front to soft in the mid-section and harder at the tail, this transition should be smooth, blending one into the other. The reason the mid-section is soft is that it allows the board to pivot around the centre and not trip or stick on the rail. Some boards will have a tucked-under edge from nose to tail.

Underwater profiles

Most boards now tend to have one (a), two (b) or four (c) concaves shaped into the underside of the hull, together with some 'V' in the tail section. A 'V' in the mid-section of a short board acts like a daggerboard, helping up-wind performance, whereas some V in the tail helps the transition from rail to rail during turns. As with the rail section, the bottom shape changes along its length in a continuous flow from front to rear. The front section may be concave to give lift and stop the nose from diving when it overtakes the wave in front. The concaves in the mid-section provide most of the lift the board needs to start planing. The concaves run into a V section in the tail or a series of channels (d), creating air pockets. These provide lift to get the board on the plane. This seems to work well with a wide tail (ie, swallow-tail) in marginal wind conditions.

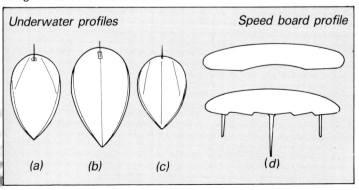

Underwater profiles   Speed board profile

(a)   (b)   (c)   (d)

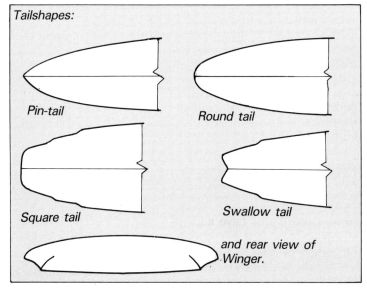

Tailshapes:

Pin-tail

Round tail

Square tail

Swallow tail

and rear view of Winger.

Tail shapes

Broadly speaking, tail shapes break down into two categories
— wide and narrow.

Wide tails are better in lighter winds. Being more 'floaty',
a wide tail means the board will get on the plane quicker,
and this makes a wide tail more suitable for heavy sailors.
Wide-tail boards can make tighter turns and are good for
small surf, and are easy to jump.

Narrow tails, on the other hand, do not have as much
buoyancy, and therefore do not plane as early — but they
do come into their own in strong winds and big waves,
when the wide tail becomes unstable and spins out. In a
high-speed turn, it is easier to dig in the tail of a narrow
board — the wide, buoyant tail will skid and cavitate.

Pin-tail or rounded pin-tail is the best narrow tail design,
ideally suited for strong winds and big surf. It will carve
high-speed, wide turns and still stay very stable throughout
the turn. The pin-tail is usually used in conjunction with a
single fin and does not have a tendency to spin out.

Round-tail. This is a wider version of the pin-tail. It works
well in more moderate wind and wave conditions, and can
be set up with small side fins or thrusters. This makes it
more versatile, good for top and bottom turns on the wave
— unlike the pin-tail which only executes good bottom turns.

Swallow-tails are a good, wide tail design with some of
the advantages of a pin-tail. By tapering the board's outline

14

down in this way (helped by using 'wingers') you get the width without drawing the tail out and increasing the board's length. These tails are good for sailors wanting a shorter board, or one usable in marginal winds. As you press the tail down in a turn, only half the swallow is in the water, and it acts like a pin-tail.

Wingers. These are cut-outs in the rails of the tail of the board and serve to reduce the tail width in the last section of the tail without reducing the width (and buoyancy) of the board under your feet.

Board fittings and accessories

Fins

Most boards either have a single large rear fin (1), or additional small side fins known as thrusters (2) placed forward either side of the main fin. The fins are held in slots known as skeg boxes, which allow some adjustment forwards or backwards with the aid of a screw-driver. Race boards and slalom boards have long single fins with cut-aways at the base of the fin or slots to reduce the possibility of cavitation (this is when the fin travelling at high speed loses contact with the water, causing an air pocket to form at the side. This breaks down the lateral resistance and the tail of the board starts to slide sideways). Smaller wave-riding boards tend either to use one fin on narrow tails or tri-fin arrangements (1) on wide tails. The idea of these is to stop 'spin out'. This occurs when the board is banked in a

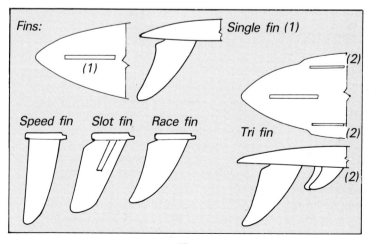

Fins: Single fin (1) (1) (2)

Speed fin   Slot fin   Race fin   Tri fin   (2)   (2)

turn and the fin pops out of the water. By adding thrusters at the side, you still keep a fin in contact with the water.

You move the fins back for better control and directional stability and forward to make the board 'looser' and more manoeuvrable.

Foot straps

These were developed in the early 1970s by Hawaiian sailors Larry Stanley and Mike Horgan. They found them useful for ploughing through the white water of the shore break and staying in contact with the board when jumping. Apart from this, foot straps help the modern funboarder to control the board at high speed on flat water and also give him confidence. Besides their value in the air, you use the front straps to pull up the windward rail in a gybe and in other manoeuvres.

You have already seen the way the straps are laid out on the different types of board. You can't move the position of the straps on the board, but you can adjust them for individual foot sizes. You need to adjust these properly to prevent damage to your ligaments when landing from a jump with your feet in the straps. There is now a trend on race boards to have double foot straps for better beating upwind.

Mast track plus daggerboard

You will find both these features on the longer race and all-round boards. They are designed to allow the board to sail at its optimum on all points of sailing — in a race perhaps.

The mast track is recessed into the hull with a foot pedal at the rear, protruding above the deck. The track, and therefore the position of the mast along the length of the board is locked unless the pedal is depressed, allowing you to vary the position while sailing.

The daggerboard can also be adjusted from being fully down to being completely retracted into the hull. You use it fully down for beating upwind and retracted for the rest of the time. There is usually a rubber gasket underneath to prevent the water spraying up through the board.

In conjunction with the daggerboard, the mast foot is pushed right forward for beating upwind. This forces the nose of the board down, producing a longer wetted area and improving up-wind performance, and allowing the rider to hang his weight on the sail. This in turn enables a larger sail area to be handled. After retracting the daggerboard, the mast foot is moved right back, reducing the wetted area, allowing the sailor to stand further back and the board will

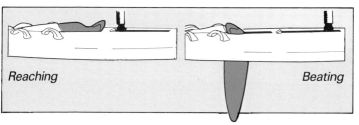

Reaching   *Beating*

plane under control on its rear half. The effect of moving the
mast track and daggerboard is to give a long board for
pointing upwind and a short board for reaching.

Sail dynamics and theory

Sail design and construction, like that of boards, have gone
through a period of rapid development. Fortunately, they
have now stabilized, and sail-makers can concentrate on fine
tuning and detailing rather than on radical changes in shape
year after year.

Construction

Manufacturers use a variety of materials in constructing their
sails, often with different trade names, made from PVC,
Polyester and Nylon. The materials are made into woven
fabric, sheets of polyester film or a combination of the
woven fabric, laminated either on to one piece of film or
sandwiched between two pieces of film (this is known as a
three-ply laminate). These have a variety of exotic names
such as Trilam, Rip Stop Mylar, K Film and Teforan.

Page 18 shows the layout of a modern sail made up of
several panels using different materials for different parts of
the sail. This one has six panels.

Theory

The explanation of how a sail works is often over-simplified
as follows. The air flowing from the mast around the back
of the sail (leeward side) has further to travel than airflow in
front (windward side). This creates a pressure difference as
the leeward flow speeds up to catch up with the windward
low. The sail is therefore sucked along rather than blown. In
fact, as the sail is so thin there is very little difference in the
distances travelled. The forward motion created is probably
more a combination of this suction along with deflection.
The sail deflects the air flow one way, creating an opposite
effect the other way — known as lift.

Design

Let us first consider the leading edge of the sail — the one presented to the wind — the luff. Some sails have short battens which end before they reach the mast, giving a 'soft' sail (a).

A 'rotational sail' (b) is constructed with full-length battens which fit tightly against the mast, which is in a narrow mast sleeve and rotates from side to side as you change tack. Another alternative is a sail with full-length battens fitting into a wide mast sleeve, held in place by plastic 'camber-inducers' (c). There used to be a great deal of discussion about how you could cut down the turbulence caused in the shadow of a circular mast on the windward side by presenting a smooth leading edge of a wing-shaped mast. This led to the development of rotational sails, but their real advantage, especially when camber-induced, is to hold the shape of the curve in the sail. This camber dictates the use of the sail. A flatter forward draft is less powerful, so is suitable for high wind or wave sailing (d), whereas a full, deep shape with the draft further back, produces a more powerful racing sail for less windy conditions (e). Slalom and more recreational sails would have a medium fullness, positioned

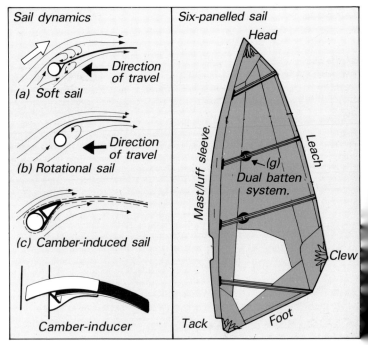

Sail dynamics

Direction of travel
(a) Soft sail

Direction of travel
(b) Rotational sail

(c) Camber-induced sail

Camber-inducer

Six-panelled sail

Head

Mast/luff sleeve.

Leach

(g)
Dual batten system.

Clew

Tack   Foot

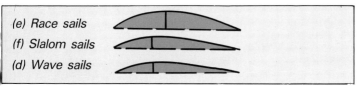

(e) Race sails
(f) Slalom sails
(d) Wave sails

somewhere between the above two(f). In fact, sail designers do not use completely 'soft' sails. They are rather a combination of full-length battens in the head and foot of the sail and short battens in the main body. The trend now is to have a twin-batten sleeve arrangement, allowing you to use either full-length or short battens. These are known as 'dual-batten systems' (g). The idea here is to make the sail more versatile. Full-length battens give you speed and acceleration on the flat, but wave-sailors want to be able to depower the sail while coming down a wave into a bottom turn, so they use the sail in soft mode for wave sailing.

Camber-inducers are not always suitable for wave sailing, but are good for racing on all points of sailing. However, if you're a recreational sailor, you should bear in mind that the camber-induced sail is fiddly to rig up and difficult to water start due to the wide luff sleeve filling up with water. The opposite is true of a narrow luff tube used on a rotational or dual-battened sail.

Sail shape

Now let's take a look at the outline shape of the sail. The 'aspect ratio' is the relationship between its height and

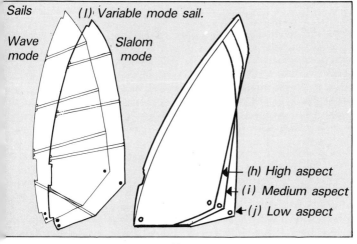

Sails (l) Variable mode sail.

Wave mode

Slalom mode

(h) High aspect
(i) Medium aspect
(j) Low aspect

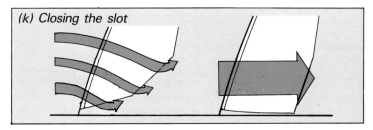

(k) Closing the slot

width. High aspect is good for high-speed planing but does not give good acceleration at low speed to get you on to a plane. This makes it suitable for speed sailing (h). Low aspect gives good acceleration on to a plane and is more powerful at lower speeds. This type of sail is used for racing and slalom (i). Medium aspect has good, all-round acceleration and is suitable for recreational and all-round use (j).

Racing and speed sails now have their foot made as close to the deck as possible. This is known as 'closing the slot'. You lose efficiency when air flows under the sail, so by careful shaping of the foot, the bottom batten is made to seal the sail to the deck when the mast is inclined (k).

In conclusion, when you choose a sail, you must decide on the conditions and the type of sailing you will use it for. A flat wave sail is no good if you never sail on the sea, and a racing sail will do you no favours in high surf. You are probably going to need at least two sizes of sail, so why not consider a compromise recreational sail which most manufacturers offer in their range. Avoid extremes in design, tell your dealer what features you require and, above all, go for quality of manufacture and design. Then make sure you look after it.

There is currently a new style developing for the recreational sailor who needs an all-round sail. Rather than having to carry several 'quivers' of sails for all disciplines, there is a new design known as the 'variable mode sail' (l). Apart from adjustable head and dual-batten system, it has a removable camber-inducer, so that the sail can be used in rotational mode without the inducer as well as in soft mode. A further development is a dual eyelet system for downhauling with a stiffened drop skirt. For waves, the lower tack eyelet is used, giving a higher clew and boom angle, while automatically flattening the head for easier handling. For speed and slalom use, the upper tack eyelet is used to form a drop skirt and lower clew. Eyelet positioning allows more fullness of the head and twist for acceleration.

Tuning the board and rig

Finding the best position for the variable elements of your board is a matter of experimentation. Give each position a good trial sail before you change it, and you will end up with a good understanding of your equipment. Make notes and even small marks on your board (mast, extension, boom, etc) with an indelible pen.

Mast base position

On a long board with a sliding track, you can adjust as you sail, but on a shorter board you must set the position before leaving the beach. If you move the base forward, you get smoother, drawn-out turns. The board will point higher up-wind and sailing in choppy water becomes more manageable. If you move the base backwards, you get sharper turns but the tail will bounce more — not a problem in flat water or smooth, small waves. As a general rule, position the base further forward for larger sails, further back for small sails. Begin by standing the board on its tail and set the mast base level with your nose.

Fin position

Sliding the fin backwards makes the board controllable and stable in a straight lines. Moving it forward makes the board more manoeuvrable and 'looser' for tight turns. Start by placing your fin so that its tip is about 10 cm from the tail of the board.

The rig

Setting a modern rig is quite straightforward, apart from dealing with some camber-inducers which can be a bit fiddly. Use your foot against the mast foot to downhaul the sail to put a curve in the mast and pull out horizontal creases in the luff of the sail.

Outhaul the sail by using pulleys and cleats, usually built into the end of the boom. This should remove any vertical creases. Push in all the full-length battens and secure tightly. Wrinkling along the batten sleeves means the battens are not tensioned enough. Take care not to over-tension the battens in the foot of the sail, or it may not rotate. Allow the wind to fill the sail and check the battens rotate freely. If not, check the downhaul pressure again — it may be too much.

CHAPTER TWO

Launching your board from the beach

It can be very easy to damage your equipment in the shore break, so good technique leaving the beach is essential — especially when there is heavy dumping of waves on to the beach.

Launching a long board (in side-shore winds)

Choose a safe place to launch and lay your board down, across the wind, pointing out to sea with the sail lying to windward, clew forward.

1 Pick up the mast with your front hand just above the boom and walk over the board to the windward side.

2 Then, bend down and pick up the tail of the board by the leeward rail or rear foot strap, holding it on its edge. This makes it easier to slide across the sand and is less likely to damage the hull.

3 Slide the board forward into the water up to about knee depth and put both hands on to the boom, pushing the nose of the board with the rig. Pushing and pulling on the rig while walking towards the board will stop it heading up into the wind.

4 When you feel you have found the right angle of board and sail to the wind, you can step up on to the rear of the board with your back foot. Watch out for the tail sinking and the fin catching on the sea bed — for this reason you shouldn't stand too near the tail.

5 Finally, sheet in and step up on to the board with your front foot and sail out. You may need to look for a lull in any breaking waves before heading out.

Launching in off-shore winds

6 The difference with off-shore winds is that, as you push the board into the water, you hold the sail with the front hand, clew first.

Once in the water you will need to position the board more parallel to the shore before holding the boom and stepping on. This brings a further problem if there is a shore break, as the waves are hitting you side on. You need to get on to the board quickly and head out on a broad reach through the oncoming surf.

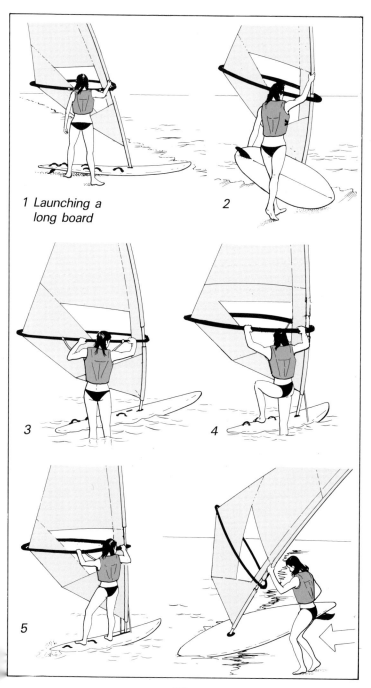

1 *Launching a long board*

2

3

4

5

Carrying and launching a short board

It is possible to carry a long board in the manner shown below if it is not too heavy, but generally speaking this method is usually used for carrying short boards, which can be transported over quite long distances. The idea is to carry your board right into the water so that you can drop it and sail away quickly.

Side-shore winds
1 Lay the short board down as before, but unlike the long board method, hold the mast with your front hand below the boom and lift up the board with your back hand by the windward front foot strap.
2 Lift the sail up over your head for walking. The wind under the sail and board should take most of its weight. Don't let the nose of the board point too high as it could become uncontrollable in gusts. Try to hold the sail up with your mast hand, but if it becomes too heavy, rest the sail on top of your head, avoiding too much pressure, particularly on the window area, which may distort. Always keep the luff of the sail pointing into the wind.
3 As you walk into the water up to knee height with the sail luffing, lower the board into the water across the wind and transfer your hands on to the boom, pushing the nose of the board off the wind via the rig.
4 Step on to the board with your back foot, sheet in, then step up with your front foot and sail away. Again, avoid sinking the tail of the board as you step on.

Off-shore winds
5 Carrying your board and rig in off-shore winds requires a different technique. Pick up the board by the front foot strap with one hand, holding the boom in the other. This time you walk between your board and rig with your back to the wind, the luff of the sail still facing the wind, but held low down for better control and handling (see figure 5).

High, gusty winds
In gusty or high winds the 'off-shore' method of carrying is the safest, even if it means walking backwards into the water (on-shore winds) or walking sideways (side-shore winds). Always hold the board and rig low and be ready to lay both down quickly in a gust rather than be flattened by your board, sail or both in a sudden gust.

Returning to the beach

Returning to the beach is really just a reversal of launching. Again, make sure to jump off your board before the skeg hits the bottom.

Long board
1 Make sure your daggerboard is fully retracted if you have one. Jump off the board to windward as you near the beach, hold the mast above the boom with your front hand, pick up the tail by the rear foot strap with your back hand and push the board on to the beach.
2 When the board is clear of the water, walk the tail of the board around, pivoting on its nose while still holding the mast, until the board is facing out to sea.
3 The sail will flip over, still in your hand, and you can drag the board backwards up the beach safely out of the shore break before laying it down.

By turning it round you will ensure the nose of the board doesn't dig in as you try to push it up the beach. You may be followed by a wave which flattens the board down hard — resulting in possible damage.

Short board
1 As with a long board, jump off before the skeg hits the bottom.
2 Holding the mast with your front hand below the boom, pick up the board by a front foot strap and, standing to windward, carry the rig above your head until you are safely out of the water.

Returning to the beach

(1)

(2)

(3)

Using a harness

A harness is a convenient way of hanging your body-weight off the boom to relieve the tension on your arms, leaving them free to control the rig while you are sailing. This allows you to sail for long periods at a time and reduces the risk of damage to the ligaments in your wrists and elbows.
However, you shouldn't use it to overcome bad technique in handling the rig. Therefore do not start to use a harness until you are confident about sailing without the help of one for short periods. Never sail, either with or without a harness, if you are tired.

Harnesses used only to be worn on the chest like a jacket. The fashion now is to have them low down, attached to a waist-band or lower on a 'nappy' (see Figs. 1-3). These are

Fig 1. **Chest harness** with the hook high up, favoured by wave-sailors. The V-shaped hook stops the line from tangling.

Fig 2. **Waist harness** with a mid-position hook, good for recreational/wave sailing

Fig 3. **Nappy/seat harness**, preferred by course racers and speed freaks. Also suitable for recreational sailing.

suitable for recreational sailing and reduce the likelihood of being catapaulted forward over the rail if you are caught off balance in a gust. Low harnesses are used in course racing and speed trials, but hard-core wave-sailors are returning to chest harnesses because they are easier to hook in and out of quickly in tight manoeuvres. All harnesses distribute the weight evenly by attaching the hook to a spreader bar made of plastic or light alloy. The hook is V-shaped to prevent the lines from wrapping themselves around and 'locking' you to the boom after a catapault — a potentially dangerous situation. With a V, the lines will always slide outward and release.

The harness lines are attached to the boom by means of adjustable velcro straps. This prevents the lines from wearing out the boom grip material.

In order to protect the rope from wearing as the loop slides inside the hook, thread a piece of narrow, flexible plastic tubing, about one-third of the length of the line, over the lines so it rests around about the middle, where the hook would be. This has the advantage of weighting the lines down and so stopping them from inadvertently flipping

Fig 4. **Correct positioning** *Your arms should be almost extended, both taking equal pressure. Lean out, letting your body-weight counterbalance the rig, leaving your arms free to control the boom.*

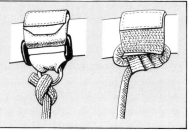

Fig 5. **Harness lines**
To hook in, swing the line towards you. To hook out, pull the boom towards you and let the line drop out of the hook.

over the boom when not in use, so that when you next come to hook in, they are too short.

Adjusting your harness lines

Obviously the length of the loop in the harness lines depends on the height of the boom in relation to your harness hook position. Leave some spare line coming off the straps in case you need to lengthen them later. Generally, you will need longer lines for long boards. Short lines will only let the rig sail more upright, so are suitable for short-board sailing. Your arms should be almost straight when you are hooked in for sailing.

To find the correct position to attach the lines to the boom, balance the sail by holding the boom with only one hand. When you have found this point, attach the straps equidistantly on either side. Then hook in on the beach — the rig should stay balanced without you using your arms.

Before testing the set-up at sea, move the rear strap backward about the width of your thumb. This will compensate for the increase in apparent wind once you start sailing.

Fault-finding

You will soon know if your lines are correctly positioned once you hook in on the water. If you find too much pressure on your front hand, pulling the mast away from you, the lines are too far back on the boom. This makes it difficult to trim by sheeting out. If, on the other hand, you find you are constantly having to move your rear hand back along the boom and there is too much pressure on that arm, the lines are too far forward. You may find this happening as the wind strength increases, which results in moving the centre of effort back.

CHAPTER FOUR

Getting on to a plane

With the help of double, concave hulls, water-release edges on the rails, adjustable mast tracks, camber-induced fully-battened sails and all the other features of the modern sailboard, you would think this amazing craft would get on to a plane all by itself!

In a sport where equipment is everything, you still need two more basic ingredients — wind and the know-how to use it. The latter really sorts out the men from the boys (and, I suppose, the women from the girls). Unfortunately, it is difficult to explain in words how to trim your sail and use its advantage to get you planing. It is more of a 'feeling' you acquire with practice. One of the quickest ways to learn is to sail with people faster than you are.

Sail trim

You trim your sail by sheeting out (letting your back hand out) until the sail begins to luff. Then you sheet in a little to stop the luffing (pull your back hand). If you sheet in too much, you stall the sail. This movement, in conjunction with raking the mast backwards and forwards, is 'trimming the sail'. This, of course, is a rather slow technique for a high-speed sport, but eventually you will get to 'feel' that your sail is trimmed correctly and it will become natural.

Planing

Planing is lifting the front of your board up out of the water on to a pocket of air, just leaving the rear section skimming across the surface of the water. You have to get into this mode for most of the exciting funboard manoeuvres.

In lighter winds (generally you need at least a force 3 to get the board planing), you are standing rather forward on the board. Look out for a gust of wind and, as it hits you, quickly trim the sail and then, as the board comes up on to a plane, move your feet further back to avoid the nose going down. If it's a strong gust, get at least your front foot into the front strap to avoid being pulled over the front of the board by the sail.

You don't necessarily have to be in the foot straps for

planing. In light winds your feet may be just in front of the straps as too much weight on the tail may sink it and you will come off the plane. Alternately, in strong winds, it may be safer to hold the sail, not quite trimmed, while you get your feet in the straps, then quickly trim the sail to accelerate the board on to a plane. Lean out, keeping the sail upright to maintain speed.

Strong gusts of wind when you are planing used to be a problem with soft sails. The effect was suddenly to move the draft in the sail backwards, heading the board upwind — or worse still, catapulting you over the front of the board. Fortunately, fully-battened sails maintain their shape far better in the gusts, making them more comfortable to sail in wild conditions.

Fig 1. Good stance
on a race board.

Fig 2. Good stance
on a slalom board

Fig 3. Good stance
on a speed board

CHAPTER FIVE

Sailing on a long board

A long board of 320-380 cm with an adjustable mast track and daggerboard is two boards rolled into one. It can be used to 'blast around on' or for all points of sailing.

Beating

This is sailing up into the wind (a), and only a long board can do this well. You need the daggerboard fully down for maximum lateral resistance. Position the mast track forward. This, combined with your feet in the front foot straps, pushes the front of the board down on to the waterline (maximum wetted area). This gives excellent up-wind performance.

Your body should be leaning out and forward. Depress the leeward rail a little for lateral resistance, keeping your feet close together, forward on the windward rail. Some boards now have double foot straps to make this easier. The sail should be sheeted in, close to the centre-line of the board.

(a) Beating

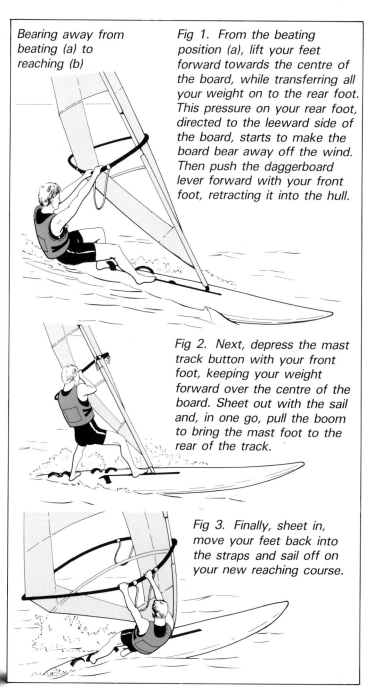

Bearing away from beating (a) to reaching (b)

Fig 1. From the beating position (a), lift your feet forward towards the centre of the board, while transferring all your weight on to the rear foot. This pressure on your rear foot, directed to the leeward side of the board, starts to make the board bear away off the wind. Then push the daggerboard lever forward with your front foot, retracting it into the hull.

Fig 2. Next, depress the mast track button with your front foot, keeping your weight forward over the centre of the board. Sheet out with the sail and, in one go, pull the boom to bring the mast foot to the rear of the track.

Fig 3. Finally, sheet in, move your feet back into the straps and sail off on your new reaching course.

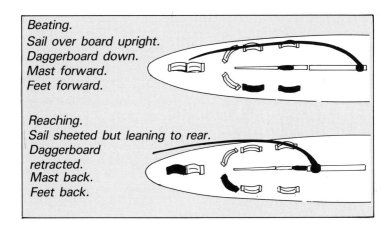

Beating.
Sail over board upright.
Daggerboard down.
Mast forward.
Feet forward.

Reaching.
Sail sheeted but leaning to rear.
Daggerboard retracted.
Mast back.
Feet back.

Reaching

Reaching (b), is sailing across the wind. By retracting the daggerboard fully and setting the mast track right back, the long board acts like a short board, planing only on its rear section. Your feet are in the straps to the rear, keeping the board flat. Lean your body out, but this time to the rear.

(b) Reaching

*Heading up
from a reach
to a beat*

Fig 4. From the reaching
position (b), you must take care
in controlling the board as you
change direction from a 'fast'
reach to a slower beat. Bring
up your back foot and position
it behind your front foot. Then
put your front foot forward
on to the mast track button,
keeping your body-weight
inclined to the windward rail.

Fig 5. Push the mast forward
with both hands on the boom
as the board continues to luff
up to windward. Swivel the
daggerboard lever back with
your front foot to lower it out
of the retracted position.

Fig 6. Move your feet over on
to the windward rail and into
the front beating straps. Lean
your body out and
forward in the beating stance.

Tacking

Tacking a long board is quite easy because it has plenty of buoyancy in front of the mast foot. Smaller boards, however, are more difficult, but even a sinker can be tacked with practice.

Tacking

With the daggerboard down and the mast foot forward in the track, start to tack.
Fig 1. Rack the mast back, pushing your rear foot back to turn the board into the wind.
Fig 2. Move forward on the board, holding the mast with your front hand and pulling on the boom with your back hand, so as to pull the clew of the sail across the centre-line of the board.
Fig 3. As the nose of the board comes into the wind, put your front foot around the front of the mast to the leeward side.

Fig 4. Keep hold of the mast and jump as quickly as you can around the front of the mast to the other side of the board, transferring your grip on the mast to your other hand as you go.

Fig 5. As soon as you are on your new side, grab the boom with your back hand, pushing the mast forward to bear off. Use your front foot to help push the board off the wind.

Fig 6. Grab the boom with your front hand, move your feet back on the boad and sail off on the new tack.

CHAPTER SIX

Foot steering

Once you have got a board planing, you can redirect it by using your feet rather than by tilting the sail back and forth. A short board travelling very fast will be very responsive to foot steering — but long boards can also be turned by this principle, albeit with more effort.

Surfers have never needed a sail to turn their boards — just the power of the waves to drive them forward. So now we use the power of the sail to get us planing and use our feet and transference of weight to change direction.

You cannot have any lateral resistance under the board, so the daggerboard — if you have one — must be fully retracted. If you are sailing a longer board with a sliding mast track, this must be in the rear position so that only the rear of the board is planing in the water.

You foot-steer keeping both feet in their straps and transferring your weight through your feet on to either the leeward or the windward rail.

Foot steering

Fig 1. Begin on a reach if you need to pump the sail to promote planing.

Fig 2. With your feet in the foot straps, push your knees forward, leaning into the direction of the turn.

Fig 3. Push down the leeward rail of the board at the tail with your rear foot while lifting the windward rail with your front foot. The board will bank over into a turn.

Fig 4. To head back up into the wind, straighten up your front leg, pushing down on the windward rail with your heel while lifting up the leeward rail with your rear foot.

Fig 5. The board then banks the other way and heads up.

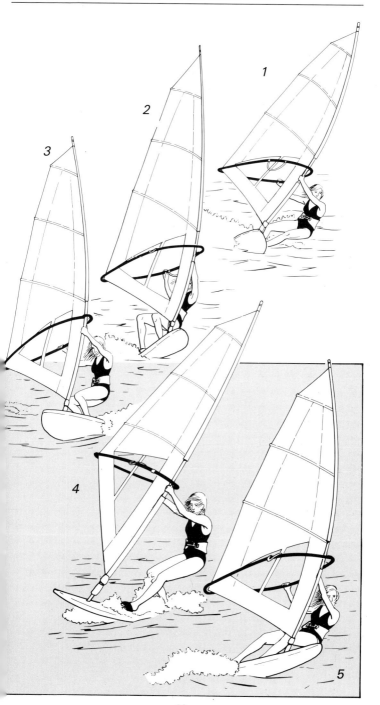

CHAPTER SEVEN

The carved gybe

Having learnt how to sail out safely through the shorebreak and get the board on to a plane, you will need to master the more important funboard manoeuvre, the carved gybe. There are several variations on the carved gybe which we will look at later, some of which are for show or fun — but here we look at it in its basic form.

The ideal board for learning the carved gybe would be a transitional short board, around 295 cm in length, and with enough buoyancy to keep you floating stationary. Conditions should be a constant force-four breeze and flat water to begin with. Your sail should be a recreational, soft or rotational sail with a good window, but not camber-induced and of a size comfortable to maintain controlled planing speed.

To achieve your first powered gybe, your board must be planing and you must have both feet in their foot-straps. Judging the correct speed takes practice. If you are under-powered, pump with your sail to promote planing. If you are overpowered, then sheet out to slow down.

If the water is a bit choppy, look for a flat area to make your turn — or a small swell can form a useful bank to help your turn, not too big though as this produces problems for the beginner (see page 77 for gybing off a wave). Always check around you quickly in case your sudden change of direction causes a collision, especially from a following board to leeward.

Now remove your rear foot from its footstrap and place it near the leeward rail between the front and back straps. Push down firmly with the ball of your back foot while pulling up the windward rail with your front foot still in its front foot strap.

This transfer of weight will cause the board to turn off the wind and initiate the turn. It is worth mentioning here that success or failure in mastering this all-important manoeuvre relies on total commitment from this point on. Hesitation or holding back will always result in a stall or wipe out.

As you continue to apply constant pressure to the inner rail, the board will accelerate due to the increase in apparent windspeed so, as it turns, trim your sail by tilting the rig back towards you.

Your knees should be bent and your body leaning into the

turn to produce a smoother gradual arc which will give you more exit speed.

You will now be approaching the down-wind section of your gybe, so move your front hand on the boom closer to the mast. As you pass through the eye of the wind, open up your sail a little by extending your back hand to maintain board-speed.

As you maintain the pressure on your back foot, you will reach a point where the sail wants to pull out of your back hand. Now let go of the boom with your back hand and let the sail pivot on your front hand while grabbing the mast with your back hand. It is important to keep the mast close to your body — almost touching your nose — so that when the sail flips, the rig is in the correct position for the tack.

Shift your weight on to your front foot a little — this will flatten out the board and stop it rounding up into the wind, and as the sail swings around, grab the other side of the boom with what was previously your front hand, still holding the mast with the other hand. Continue to transfer your weight on to your front foot, let go of the mast and grab the boom. Sheet in slowly, so as not to stall the rig.

At this point your feet will be the wrong way around and it will feel very awkward — but don't move them until you are on a plane on your new course. Then, by hanging your weight off the boom when everything else has been sorted out, you can swap your foot positions over into the straps.

Problems

You must realize that it is your feet which are making the board turn — not the sail, so you must keep digging the inside rail with your rear foot. If you ease up at any time you just end up going straight ahead and not turning. Also, you must keep the board on the plane throughout the whole gybe or you will stall. If you let go of the boom too late you will also stall the board, throwing yourself backwards into the water. Similarly, if you let go too early while the board is heading downwind, you will slow down or be thrown over the nose. Of course, with practice, you can overcome these problems until the movements become second nature.

In strong winds it is important to keep your weight low throughout the turn to stop yourself being catapulted forward. Dig in the rear inside rail even harder and lean into the turn more.

If you find yourself going too fast, ease up on the turning

circle and pull in with your back hand to stall the sail a bit if necessary.

When you are on the down-wind section, open out the sail again to regain speed. You can release the boom earlier and holding only the mast (tilted back), let the board carve around it at full planing speed.

For a successful carved gybe you must be totally committed from start to finish. Remember it is your feet which are making the board turn, not the sail. Keep the pressure constant on your rear foot and bend your knees, keeping your weight low. Tilt the mast back slightly and lean into the turn.

You are at full planing speed on a beam reach:
Fig 1. Remove your back foot out of its strap and place it on the leeward rail, applying firm pressure.
Lean into the turn, bending your knees.
Fig 2. Sheet in the sail to control the turn.
Fig 3. In the down-wind section, begin to open out your sail and move your front hand nearer the mast.
Fig 4. Let go with your back hand and grab the mast.

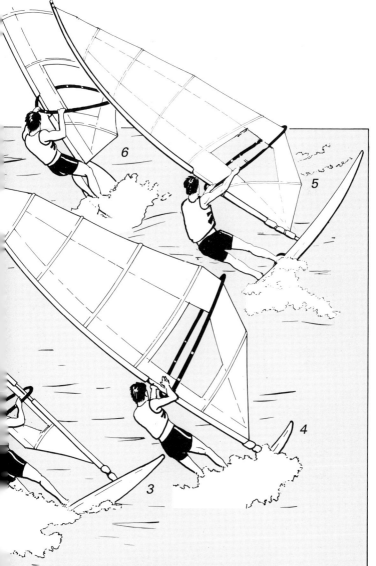

The sail pivots around the front of the mast.

Fig 5. Grab the boom on the new side, easing the pressure off your rear foot.

Fig 6. Move your front hand off the mast on to the boom, trimming the sail with your back hand. Finally, change your feet over into the correct position.

Gybing boom to boom

If you have mastered the basic method of gybing, now is the time to try a slightly more advanced technique, which involves momentarily taking both hands off the rig. It used to be called a 'no-handed gybe', but it is really best described as 'gybing boom to boom'. Once learnt, you may prefer it to the standard method, as it makes the transition rather more fluid and has the added attraction of looking rather smooth.

Fig 1. Begin your turn as described in the standard method, that is, at full planing speed, take your back foot out of its strap and depress the leeward rail — lift up the windward rail with your front foot in the foot straps. Bend both knees, leaning into the turn. Trim the sail according to your speed and control.

Fig 2. Coming into the down-wind section, move your front hand nearer the mast, holding the boom with an underhand grip, almost just on your fingertips.

Fig 3. Continuing to carve the board around with your feet, release your back hand by throwing the boom away forward (still holding it with your front hand) as you approach the dead down-wind position.

Fig 4. With the sail now clew forward, down-wind in neutral, tilt the mast backwards towards you. In one motion, let go your front hand, at the same time reaching over with your other hand to grab the boom near the mast on the other side.

Fig 5. Ease the pressure off your rear foot to begin straightening out of the turn, and grab the boom with what is now the back hand, and sheet in.

Fig 6. When you are all set up on your new tack with the sail trimmed, your board still on the plane, change your feet into the correct position.

CHAPTER EIGHT

Water starts

Water starting is one of the quickest ways to get up and sailing after a fall. In fact, on a low-buoyancy short board which you cannot uphaul, it is the only way. Therefore it's a very important technique to master. You should practise on a board you can uphaul (if necessary in a shallow bay or harbour where you can walk the sail around, rather than swim it to begin with). Never learn on a sinker, out of your depth or without assistance at hand.

A board of about 320 cm with a short boom on the sail on flat water and a low, force-four breeze would be ideal.

The idea of a waterstart is to use the power of the wind to lift you up on to the board in a position to sail away. Once mastered, it is considerably easier than uphauling your sail, especially in strong winds in choppy conditions when uphauling is nearly impossible.

Unfortunately, when you fall off your board, you and your sail don't always land in the most convenient position. However, let's consider the most straightforward situation first.

Your board is roughly pointing in the direction of the wind, and the sail is on the windward side of the board, mast to the front, clew to the rear.

1 Swim, holding the mast until it is at right angles to the wind, exposing the maximum luff area to give lift. With your

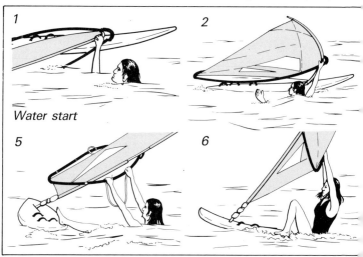

Water start

back to the wind, hold the mast above the boom with your front hand and try to lift the mast as high as you can, treading water with your feet and paddling with your other hand.

2 If it is not coming out of the water, swim to windward so the mast tip is pointing into the wind. Then the clew should pop out of the water.

3 You can now grab hold of the boom with both hands holding it high out of the water. Your board will now be at 90° to the direction of the wind. If you are using a rotational fully-battened sail, it may be curved the wrong way at this point so you need to give it a sharp pump-like action to invert it and set the sail correctly. Now you can trim it above the water as if you were sailing.

4 Now push the mast forwards so that the nose of the board points downwind towards a beam reach.

5 Next, place your back foot on the tail of the board.

6 Then pull the tail of the board towards you to windward, with your foot still keeping the sail trimmed. Sheet out with your back hand, bending your knee to keep your body near to the board. Then with straight arms and your other leg treading water, the sail will begin to lift you up on to the board.

7 As you rise out of the water, keeping your centre of gravity low, the board begins to move forward. Bring up your front foot and you are off.

8 In light winds you may need to pump the sail to pull you out of the water. In a gust you need to lean the mast forward as you come up.

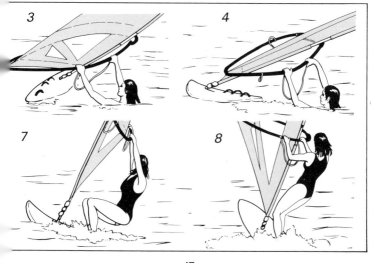

The complications

Water starting is often difficult to begin with and requires perseverance to master. You may run into the following problems:

● **The clew end keeps digging into the water.** Push the mast down just under the water.

● **You cannot raise the mast enough to get the wind under it.** Hold the mast further along its length, even by the tip, and raise it, pointing into the wind. Then swim back along its length, jumping your hand along the mast while holding it out of the water until you get back to the boom.

● **The board keeps rounding up into the wind.** Swim towards the board, pushing the rig forward.

● **The board nose-dives when you have your back foot on the tail.** The sail is over-powered, so sheet out with your back hand.

How about what to do when the sail has not landed in a convenient position? Using the theory that it is usually easier

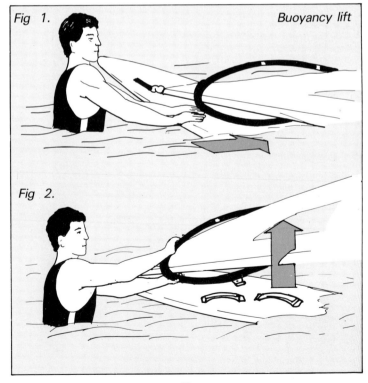

Fig 1.   *Buoyancy lift*

Fig 2.

to move the board around in the water than the sail, you can use the buoyancy of the board to raise the sail. Pushing the board as close to the mast as possible, at right angles to the wind, sink the tail of the board under the lower boom and it will lift the mast, allowing the wind to get under the sail (figs 1, 2).

● **Sail to windward but clew first.** (i) Swim, holding the tip of the mast towards the tail of the board. (ii) Swim to the clew end and lift it up so the wind flips it over. (iii) Now you are in a position to begin your water start.

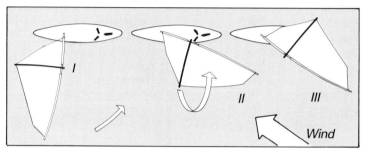

● **Sail is on the wrong side and the clew the wrong way around.** (i) Holding the clew, swim it towards the tail of the board pushing the tail around a bit. (ii) When the clew is pointing into the wind, lift it so it flips over. (iii) Now swim the mast to the back of the board holding it just above the boom. (iv) Sink the tail of the board under the submerged boom and 'buoyancy lift' the rig.

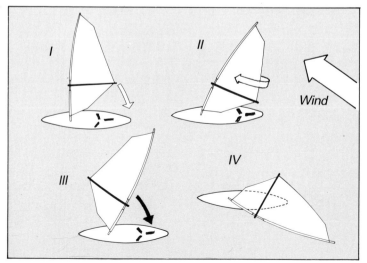

Clew-first water starts

When you have got the hang of water starts you can
attempt clew-first water starts. These have the advantage of
not needing to reposition or flip the rig in the water and so
save time and effort in swimming the rig around.

A typical situation for the clew-first water start is when
you 'blow' your gybe and fall off, having turned the board
but not yet flipped the sail. You end up in the water,
possibly still holding the boom and rig out of the water. You
can quickly pull yourself up, flip the rig and sail away.

Say the situation is as it was in (i). Hold the mast
above the boom and push the board and rig downwind. Lift
the mast, treading water as before. Put your back foot on to
the board and let the wind lift you up clew first. (ii) When

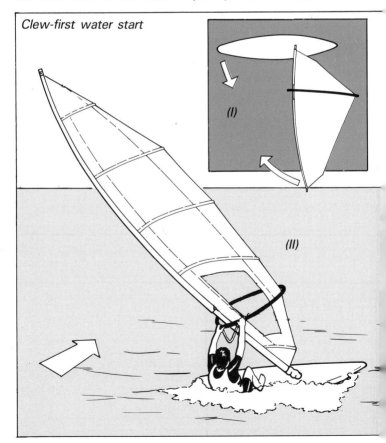

Clew-first water start

(I)

(II)

you are up with both feet on the board and stable, let go with your front hand and, as the sail flips around the front of the board, grab the mast with your front hand to hold yourself against the wind and push forward with your front foot to point the board off the wind (iii).Move your hand on to the boom, sheet in and sail away. When you are standing up on the board it is positioned across the wind and stationary. Therefore, if you are on a low buoyancy board, you need to flip the sail quickly and get under way as soon as possible before you sink.

The great thing about the clew-first water start is that, when perfect, you can take a fall and then be up and away in a matter of seconds. Apart from looking very impressive, it is also an essential survival aid when you fall off in front of heavy breaking surf.

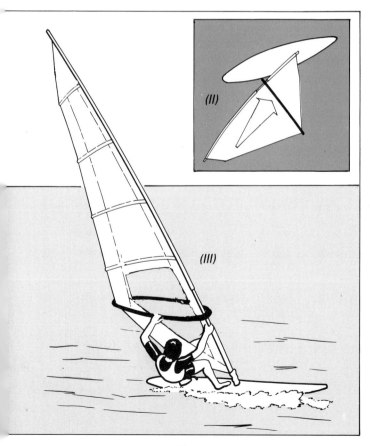

(II)

(III)

CHAPTER NINE

Advanced Windsurfing

Duck gybe

The duck gybe was a rather clumsy boom-to-sail-to-boom trick when it first appeared, but now top sailors have refined it to the smooth, high-speed boom-to-boom transition it is today.

It is, of course, a variation of the basic carved gybe, but carried out faster due to the sail being driven by the wind throughout almost all the gybe. This helps keep the board speed up to carry out the whole manoeuvre on the plane.

Duck gybe
Fig 1. As before, start your gybe at full planing speed, under control on a reach. Take your rear foot from its strap and dig in the inside rail.
Fig 2. Pulling the clew of the sail in towards the centre-line of the board, move your front hand over the other one to grab the boom near the rear end. Let go with what was previously your back hand.
Fig 3. As you carve through the down-wind position, pull the clew over your head, pulling the boom backwards and grab the front of the other boom with your free hand.

Fig 4. Continue to dig in the inside rail and grab the boom with what is now your back hand.

Fig 5. Still carving, ease your hands into the correct position on the new side of the boom and begin to sheet in slowly.

Fig 6. With the board almost round, begin to flatten out and swap over your foot positions, moving your back foot forward first. Sheet in to trim the sail for your new track.

Points to watch for.

As you duck under the clew of the sail, keep pulling the boom backwards, as the mast has a tendency to fall forward.

Don't sheet in too early. Let the board carve all the way around first.

One-handed gybes

One-handed gybes, apart from being a bit of showmanship, have no advantage over regular gybes. However, you can only carry them out if you are in complete control of the manoeuvre. So, from this aspect, they are a satisfying trick to practise.

The idea is to drag your hand nonchalantly in the water as your carve through the mid-section of the turn. The longer you drag it in the water, the cooler it looks. However, it takes some time to perfect, so it is best to practise out of sight of fellow sailors.

One-handed gybes must be carried out rather more quickly than the basic gybes — and with total commitment. Leaning out to trail your hand makes the board turn more sharply and slows it down. Try crouching down to begin with. As you improve, you should be able to lean out straight-legged.

One-handed gybe

Fig 1. Begin your turn as normal by taking your foot from its strap. Dig the inside rail in. Move your front hand close to the mast.
Fig 2. As you approach the down-wind position, let go with your back hand, lean out and drag that hand in the water.
Fig 3. Reach back up, grasping the mast with the hand which was in the water to control the rig, letting go with the other hand.

Fig 4. Put pressure on your front foot to flatten out the board. Still maintaining speed, reach out and sheet in the new side of the rail, ready to change feet and sail away.

One-handed duck gybe

The difference here is that you drag your hand as you go
under the clew, instead of going straight for the other side
of the boom. Take care not to lose control of the sail as you
drag your back hand in the water. Try to keep your centre
of gravity low to begin with, flipping the sail over as upright
as possible.

One-handed duck gybe

*Fig 1. Begin the approach as for a normal duck gybe — but
faster. Start carving a turn and bring your front hand over to
grab the back of the boom. Then let go with your front
hand.*

*Fig 2. Duck under the clew of the sail and bend down,
dragging your hand in the water.*

*Fig 3. As the board turns faster now, quickly pull up your
water hand to grab the front of the boom on the other side.*

*Fig 4. Let go with your back hand, transferring it to the
back of the boom on the new side. At the same time,
begin to flatten out the board, ready to sheet in. Transfer
your feet and sail off on the new tack.*

Scissor or snap gybe

Fig 1. From a reach, fall off the wind a little and put both feet on to the tail of the board and push down hard.

Fig 2. Begin to put more pressure on the inside leg so that the board begins to pivot on the tail. As it does, pull the sa across the board, leaning the mast back to slow you down.

Fig 3. Continue to push hard with your inside leg with the board's nose up in the air. The board turns just on its tail.

Scissor or snap gybe

This gybe is used to turn very quickly without having to lose ground downwind. You snap or pivot the board sharply on its tail while virtually stationary, as opposed to carving down wind some distance. It is particularly useful if you are in a tight spot and need to turn quickly, but have no room to manoeuvre — for example when drifting towards rocks on the 'inside' (near the shore break). You need to gybe to get out and make some headway up wind, but you dare not drift any more by carving in an arc downwind. The snap gybe is also used to good effect by slalom racers, who need to turn sharply to gain advantage when rounding a buoy. This is one of the few gybes which is not carried out on the plane throughout.

As you pass through the eye of the wind, start to open out the sail, letting the mast come up.

Fig 4. When the sail is clew first, let go with your back hand and use it to grab the mast while changing the position of your feet.

Fig 5. The sail flips over the front of the board. You grab the boom on the new side, sheet in and sail away.

Monkey gybe

Monkey gybe

This is an interesting 'fun' version of the gybe, which looks very fluid when performed correctly.

Start the gybe in the normal manner, on the plane. Take your rear foot out of the foot strap and place it on the leeward rail — but this time up near the front foot straps. Press down hard to initiate the carve. Then put the other foot just in front of (and around) the foot of the mast — again on the leeward rail. As you step forward, backwind the sail and let your body and sail rotate around through the eye of the wind, releasing your clew hand to allow your body to swing around the mast. Then continue to sail out of the gybe in the normal manner.

The 360 gybe.

The 360

The 360 is more a piece of showmanship than a manoeuvre as it does not serve any useful purpose since you end up travelling in the same direction as you started — however, it's fun to do and scores good points with onlookers on the beach — especially those who can't do it.

The ideal conditions are flat water and a good upper force-4 to 5 wind. Your board should be a maximum of 285 cms, and ideally around 270 with a short boom, preferably not with a rotational sail for learning. Speed is of the essence for this trick, so a small, fast-turning board is good, but it needs some buoyancy to help you through the middle of your turn.

The 360 technique
1 Begin at full planing speed as fast as you can handle — but still in control. Take your back foot out of the strap and dig in the inside rail, carving a smooth, wider-than-normal gybing radius.

2 Keep your weight forward, leaning on to the rig as you pull the back end of the boom over the tail of the board. Continue to carve right around.

3 Stretch your arms out straight so that your sail is hovering just above the water with the mast tip pointing into the wind. Now is the crucial point when the foot of the sail is almost touching your shins. It is not enough just to push down the sail, you must find the point of balance where your weight just equalizes the pressure of the wind now under your sail — or you will be thrown backwards over the board or fall forwards on to the rig. With good technique you can keep the board turning around by maintaining the pressure on the inside rail.

4,5,6 and 7 Still with your front foot in its strap, pull the sail up over you, pushing the board around with your feet until you are facing the original direction of travel. Then sail away.

To begin with it may help to take your front foot out of the strap and put it forward behind the mast, pushing forward as you pull over the rig and quickly hang your weight as the board moves forward again.

Aerial gybe

The aerial gybe is a means of changing direction by rotating your board around in a low-level jump. Although it's not a very smooth-looking transition, it is a very impressive manoeuvre to pull off. Like the scissor gybe, it is useful for turning round in a tight spot.

Look out for a small wave and hit it at full speed. As you lift off in the air, take your feet out of the straps and use

The Aerial gybe

them to push the tail of the board around, so that its nose points downwind. Try to keep the tail up higher than the nose. When you have got the board around, put your back foot ahead of the foot strap to windward. Land, nose first, with your board and legs in front of you. You will land in the water bottom first, hanging on to the sail at the side. Keep the wind in the sail and let it pull you up like a clew-first water start. Once you are up, flip the sail, change your foot positions and sail away.

CHAPTER TEN

Wave-jumping

Wave-jumping does not only relate to the spectacular photos you see in every windsurfing magazine, taken in exotic locations with enormous waves. This aspect of the sport is within the capabilities of any shorter-board sailors who have learnt to handle their boards in a force-4 wind. Nor do you need giant ocean waves. You can get a good jump off one-foot high chop on a lake if the wind is right.

Wind direction

The best conditions for wave (or chop) jumping are a minimum force-4 wind strength, preferably at right angles to the direction the waves are travelling. If you are sailing from a beach with the waves coming parallel to the shore line, the best wind is 'side-shore' — coming from left or right. Next best is 'side-on', next 'side-off', but never off-shore or on-shore, when you would be hitting the waves broadside, and jumping would be hopeless.

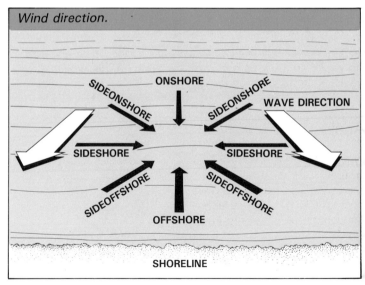

Wind direction.

Getting out through the breaking waves (or white water) on the inside is going to be the first problem to overcome. The white water foam slows the board down just when you are trying to build up speed for a jump. Side-shore winds are not such a problem. You usually have enough speed to lift up the nose of the board at the last second, allowing the aerated water to flow quickly under the board. If the wind is side on-shore, you will be sailing out at an angle — so head up at the last second to jump the foam. Bear away directly after you are clear to build up speed again.

In side off-shore conditions your are at an angle to the waves. Bear off the wind at the last second in order to hit the foam head on. Then head up again to regain speed when you are through.

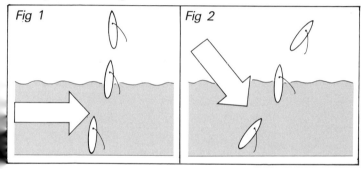

Fig 1 In side-shore winds, you are sailing into the waves on a beam reach, head on — perfect conditions for getting a good ramp to jump off at full speed.

Fig 2 In side on-shore winds, you are sailing at an angle to the waves in order to stay on beam reach. This means you will need to head up at the last moment to jump the wave.

Analysing the waves

Waves are formed far out to sea, either by storms creating ground swells or by constant wind in one direction creating wind swell. These swells travel great distances across deep oceans until they hit something shallow — such as the Continental Shelf here in Europe or coral reefs off islands which rise straight out of the sea. When the swell hits the shallows, the bottom section slows down, causing the top to overtake it, topple over and break away, forming a breaking wave. This is what we sailors like to jump and ride.

The wave starts to form as a swell and builds up a steep wave face where it peaks at the critical section and breaks away at the lip into white water.

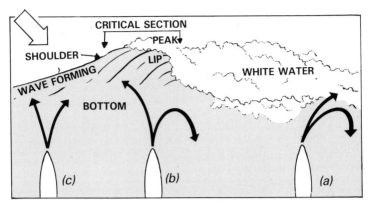

When you're confronted with a breaking wave, you must decide the best course of action to take. If you are faced with a mountain of white water (a), best gybe away from it or head for the smallest section. If you are approaching the peak (b), gybe away or try to go for the less critical section. The best position is facing the shoulder of the forming wave, (c), where you can jump over the swell or head for the steep section for a high jump.

You should attack steep faces and white water straight on — swells and chops can be tackled at an angle.

If you fall (wipe out) in front of a breaking wave, try to water start and get out of the situation. If you don't have time, try to swim the tip of your mast to face the oncoming white water. If possible, try to sink the tip under the water and hang on to it as the wave passes over.

Jumping small waves

Jumping small waves

Now for the basic technique for jumping — starting on a small wave, swell or chop.

Fig 1 Begin at full speed on a beam reach if possible, both feet in the straps, and look for the steepest ramp from which to take off. Hook out of your harness.

Fig 2 Luff up slightly as you approach the wave. As the nose rises up the ramp, keep the sail sheeted in. Your knees should be slightly bent. When the nose goes up in the air, use your feet to tilt the board to leeward so that its underside faces the wind. Pulling the board up with your feet allows the wind to get under the board, giving it extra lift. Lean your body out but pull the sail towards you as if you were pulling yourself up on a cross-bar.

Fig 3 Now you are in the air, using the sail like a hang glider and leaning to windward. The nose of the board should still be pointing down wind slightly.

Fig 4 With the sail trimmed to let you descend sheeted out, the safest landing to begin with is tail first. Flatten out the board and push down with your rear foot, straightening out your front leg.

Fig 5 Let the tail land in the water, absorbing your impact by bending your knees as you land. The nose should land immediately after. Push the board off the wind slightly to get going and sheet in.

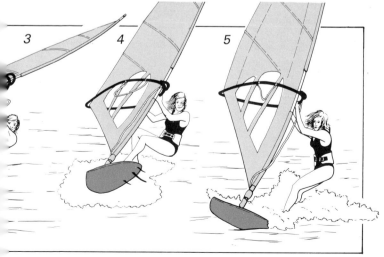

Jumping bigger waves

Once you've broken yourself in on some small waves, you can apply the same principle to larger ones. At full planing speed, hit the wave square on, both feet in the straps — and remember to hook out of your harness. Here are some of the variations to try.

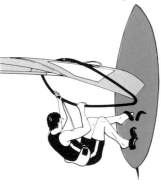

High jumps
Go for the steepest ramp you can see. Aim as high as possible with the nose, without going totally vertical. Keep some forward momentum going and don't lift up the tail until you reach the top of the jump.

Long jumps
If you are going for distance, look for a smaller ramp on the shoulder of the wave. Hit it at full speed — but this time, lift the tail of the board up as it leaves the water. Trim the sail to try to keep the board parallel to the water.

Tail-first landing
This is the safest way to land and probably the easiest. Push down with your back foot to get the tail down into the water first. Bend your knees to absorb the impact. Push your front foot down immediately after impact to get the nose down, ready for sailing away.

Nose-first landing

Landing nose first has the advantage, if done correctly, of allowing you to sail straight off on a plane — especially from a long jump. Keep the windward rail up slightly so that the leeward front rail hits the water first, rather than landing the board flat.

Donkey kick

Pull the tail up with your back foot, twisting your body towards the sail. Hang your weight out sideways, allowing the board to go on its edge. Try not to let the nose go downwind of the tail on landing.

Upside-down jumps

Take off from a steep section of the wave, leaning your body back as you go up the face. Pull up hard with your front foot. As the tail leaves the wave, use your back foot to kick it up over your head and into the wind.

Spin out

To begin with you may experience the tail spinning out sideways when you land on it. Try to kick the tail out into the wind when you land so that the nose points downwind. This alleviates the pressure on the fin and reduces spin-out.

Bailing out

If things go wrong in the air and it looks like you are going to land badly and hurt yourself or the board — bail out. Quickly check there is nothing below you, then get your feet out of the straps and push the board away with your feet and the rig with your hands pushing on the boom. Push the board and rig downwind so they blow away from you.

Forward role

This was originally known, rather dramatically, as the 'killer loop' — until it became apparent that most advanced sailors lived through it. However, you should be careful with any loop or roll manoeuvre. Things can go wrong, especially when you get disorientated by going around in the air. You can now buy light-weight crash-helmets to wear in the water — and even body pads. Remember — take care — this is an advanced trick to try after you've mastered upside-down jumps and aerial gybes.

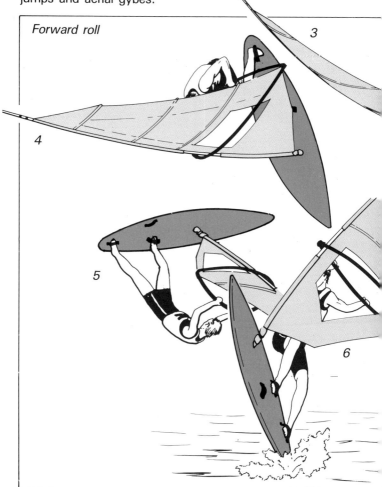

Forward roll

Look for a good small wave, not too steep.(1) Bear away from the wind at full speed as you hit the ramp.(2) As you take off into the air, sheet in with your back hand and push out with your front hand.(3) Lean forward, bending your knees and tucking your body over the boom and into the sail.(4) Keep your centre of gravity forward as you propel yourself over the boom through the roll.

(5) As you come out of the roll, your body should return to the vertical position. (6) Pull hard on the rig, bending your knees to absorb your impact as you land tail first.

Flatten the board out with your front foot and sail off.

Backward loop

Only a few years ago there was a $10,000 prize in Hawaii for the first person to complete a 360° loop in the air. Now many experienced sailors are pulling them off.

The fore-runner of the loop was the 'barrel roll' — rather like the forward roll, but rotating backward. Unlike the barrel roll, where the sail goes over in a horizontal plane, the loop goes through a completely upside down and hanging on section. Like all aerial tricks, it can be dangerous, so take care.

Backward loop

Begin the loop at full planing speed, but this time carve hard into the wave ramp at the last moment. Bringing the board into the wind helps initiate rotation — remember to keep your sail sheeted in until you are right round. Pull the board up with your front foot as you would for an upside-down jump. Keep your eye on the water as you rotate around and try not to get disorientated as you pass through the upside-down section. As you come down, transfer your weight to the back foot in order to get the tail down first. Once you are right around, sheet out and prepare for a tail-first landing.

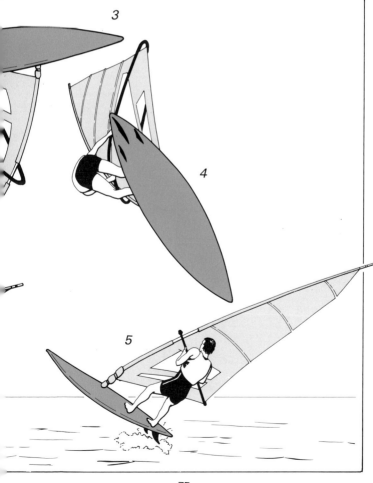

CHAPTER ELEVEN

Wave-riding

Sailing in waves is great fun — but can be potentially
dangerous, so you must abide by the rules to avoid collisions
and other accidents.

First and foremost, remember that sailboards ALWAYS
give way to surfers and body surfers, as they are less
manoeuvrable than you. Never drop into a wave which
already has surfers on it, and if there are other windsurfers,
the first one on the wave has right of way. When two
sailors go for a wave, the up-wind sailor has right of way.
As with all sailing, the board on a starboard tack (right hand
nearest the mast) has right of way. Common sense also
means you always look behind you downwind before gybing
— and if you are trying any crazy tricks, do them away from
the other wave-users.

Rock bottom

Beware of anything sharp on the sea bed — coral, rocks,
sea urchins and so on, and avoid putting your feet down.
Look out too, for rocks and coral above the water, especially
when the tide is going out. Deep waters provide flat water
to get out through — but beware — they can have 'rip
tides'. These are strong currents, feeding the water back out
to sea. Unless you are very experienced, only sail where
others are already sailing, and ask locals' advice about the
conditions, tides and prevailing currents.

Gybing on a wave

Wind direction and strength play an important part in wave-sailing. Just as for jumping, side-shore winds are the best, followed by side on-shore, then side off-shore. When you are on the water you will get the feel as to which is the best direction to travel on the wave according to the direction of the wind — but as a guide, in a side-shore wind it's best to travel in the same direction as the wind, whereas in side on-shore, you are on a good beam reach (the fastest point of sailing) when you are traversing into the side from which the wind is coming. In side off-shore winds, go with the direction of the wind.

Roller coasters

The whole point of wave-riding is to sail out through the waves — jumping them as you go — and gybe around, either outside the wave line or into the face of a wave. Then ride the wave back by 'dropping in' on the wave, sailing down the face, doing a bottom turn at the base and projecting yourself up the face again. Here you perform a top turn and come down again. Linking these top and bottom turns together in a zig-zag along the line of the wave is known as 'roller coasters'.

Gybing on the wave

This is carried out in just the same way as a regular gybe or fuck gybe, but like driving a car round a banked circuit, it is easier, as the bank and forward motion of the wave help to keep the board on the plane. Begin to carve just before you reach the wave and release your back hand early as the nose goes up the face. The sail should flip at the highest point of the turn and the wave will carry you round. You then complete the gybe normally. Keep your weight back to maintain control after the sail has flipped and as the board is picking up the momentum of the wave. If you find you are sailing out through the back of the wave, you are beginning your carve too late.

Dropping in

If you have not gybed into the wave in order to catch it, you will need to pick it up coming in from the outside — this is known as dropping in. The wave will lift up your tail and propel you forward along and down the wave at great

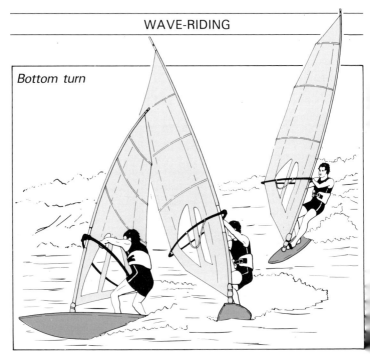

Bottom turn

speed. Try to time your entrance so the curl of the wave is breaking just behind you. If you leave it too late, the nose of the board will be forced vertically straight down the wave face — and disaster is inevitable. To avoid this, backwind the sail to stall the board by pushing the boom away from you, holding the board back from dropping in.

Bottom turns

Having come down the wave, you will want to execute a bottom turn in order to climb up the wave again. As you come to the bottom, carve away from the wind, rather like a gybe, but keeping your feet in the straps. The board will be planing very fast due to the apparent wind resulting from the board speed *and* the speed of the wave — so watch out for spin-out. Whether you draw out the turn or make it very tight, dictates the position in which you end up at the top.

Top turns

Top turns demand skill, judgement and perfect timing. A 'cutback' is a drawn-out top turn executed away from the breaking lip, which will take you back towards the critical section of the wave. Your bottom turn then powers you up the face.

As you are approaching the top, depress the inner rail, still in your straps and keeping the rig tilted back. Carve around

Cut back

the top. Flatten the board out, pushing it down with your front foot.

Slashback

You can perform a 'slashback' on the same section of the wave, just down from the lip, but this time it is a sharp turn made by putting extreme pressure on the inside rail of the tail, so making the board pivot around the top of the wave.

Off the lip

This is one of the most difficult manoeuvres to perform, especially on big waves. You depend on your bottom turn to direct you vertically up the wave face, timing it just right so the underside of the board's nose hits the lip of the wave just as it is breaking. On impact, you depress the inside rail very hard at the tail in order to pivot around, and the wave pushes you down the face. Lean back a little in order to prevent the nose of the board from diving. Take care that the breaking lip does not hit the lee side of the sail, plummeting you head first down the wave.

Aerial off the lip

This is when you hit the lip of the wave, but direct the board into the air. You then turn it in mid air by weighting the front foot and hand, directing it back down the wave.

Glossary

Apparent wind A wind experienced on a moving board. Its change of direction is produced by the speed of the board.

Back side Sailing along a wave with your back to its face.

Back winding Pushing the sail into the wind to slow the board down.

Beating Sailing up into the wind as close to the wind as possible.

Bottom turn Turning at the bottom of the wave in order to project the board back up the face of the wave.

Break Where swells hit shallow water and form breaking waves.

Beam reach Sailing at right angles to the wind. This is the fastest point of sailing.

Carve Turning the board on its inside rail.

Cavitation Air being drawn down the side of the skegs causes them to lose grip, making the tail slide sideways to leeward.

Chop Small, irregular waves.

Close out A wave which breaks along its whole length.

Cut back A fast turn at the top of the wave to direct you down the wave face.

Cross-shore Wind blowing perpendicular to the direction of the waves.

Draft The degree of maximum camber in the sail which positions the centre of effort.

Drawn-out A long, wide turn.

Drop in Getting on to the wave face for a ride.

Eye of the wind The exact direction from which the wind is coming.

Fall off To change course away from the wind.

Front side Wave-riding with your front to the wave face.

Head up To change course towards the wind.

Kick out To leave a wave before it closes out.

Leeward The opposite side to windward.

Luff up To change course into the wind.

Off the lip Hitting the breaking lip so it forces the board back down the wave face.

Peak The point at which the wave begins to break.

Plane Sailing over the surface of the water with minimum displacement at high speed.

Pumping Sheeting out then in quickly to accelerate the board artificially.

Pointing Sailing as close to the wind as possible.

Port tack Wind coming from the left side (left hand nearest the mast).

Rip A strong current caused by waves or tide.

Set Waves which come in one after the other in groups.

Shoulder The end part of the wave which has not yet broken.

Spin out To turn the board so sharply that the tail drifts sideways.

Starboard tack Wind coming from the right side (right hand nearest the mast).

Slash back A sharper cutback turn nearer to the tip.

Tacking Turning the board so that the nose goes through the eye of the wind.

Top turn Turning on the top of the wave to bring the board back down the face.

Trimming Adjusting the sail angle for the best aerodynamic efficiency.

Tube A hollow wave.

Transition A change of direction, such as a gybe.

Windward The side from which the wind is blowing.